Demonology

by

W.B. Godbey

First Fruits Press
Wilmore,
Kentucky
c2018

Demonology, By W.B. Godbey.

First Fruits Press, © 2018

ISBN: 9781621717966 (print), 9781621717973 (digital), 9781621717980 (kindle)

Digital version at http://place.asburyseminary.edu/godbey/14/

Godbey, W. B. (William Baxter), 1833-1920.
    Demonology / by W.B. Godbey... to which is added chapters on The devil and demons / by L.L. Pickett ; Demon possession in Russia / by F.B. Meyer ; The devil / by Andrew Johnson ; An angel visit / by J.M. Dustman. – Wilmore, KY : First Fruits Press, ©2018.
    pages 73; cm. 0.50
    Reprint. Previously published: Louisville, KY : Pickett Publishing Co., c1902.
    ISBN: 9781621717966 (pbk.)
    1. Demonology. 2. Spiritual warfare. I. Title. II. Pickett, L. L. (Leander Lycurgus), 1859-1928. III. Meyer, F. B. (Frederick Brotherton) 1847-1929. IV. Johnson, Andrew, 1975- V. Dustman, J. M.

BT975.G45 2018   231.3

Cover design by Jon Ramsay

asburyseminary.edu
800.2ASBURY
204 North Lexington Avenue
Wilmore, Kentucky 40390

First Fruits
THE ACADEMIC OPEN PRESS OF ASBURY SEMINARY

First Fruits Press
The Academic Open Press of Asbury Theological Seminary
204 N. Lexington Ave., Wilmore, KY 40390
859-858-2236
first.fruits@asburyseminary.edu
asbury.to/firstfruits

DEMONOLOGY

BY

REV. W. B. GODBEY, A. M.

Commentator and Translator of the New Testament
and Author of Sundry Books, to which is
added chapters on

THE DEVIL AND DEMONS
by Evangelist L. L. Pickett,

DEMON POSSESSION IN RUSSIA.
by Rev. F. B. Meyer.

THE DEVIL
by Rev. Andrew Johnson,

AN ANGEL VISIT
by Rev. J. M. Dustman.

•◁••◁•

PRICE: Paper, 15c; Cloth, 30c.

•◁••◁•

PICKETT PUBLISHING CO.,

Louisville, Ky.   Greenville, Texas.

1432 Franklin St., St. Louis, Mo.

DEMONOLOGY

CHAPTER I.

VASTITUDE OF THE CELESTIAL UNIVERSE.

Dr. Dick tells us seventeen hundred millions of glowing suns, many of them much larger than ours, have already been discovered. Our sun is attended by ten great worlds, of which this is one of the smallest, Neptune being 60 times the size of the earth, Uranus 80, Saturn 1,100, and Jupiter 1,400 times the size of this world. These worlds are in full view. We gaze on them every clear night. When viewed with powerful telescopes, they thrill us with wonder and flood us with bewildering edification, and anon, with a longing to fly away and visit them, ranging from world to world and exploring the wonders of omnipotence with adoring appreciation. On the hypothesis, which is quite plausible, that all these suns are attended by retinues of worlds, doubtless as large as ours, it gives us the enormous number of one billion, one hundred and seventy millions of bright, celestial worlds. Then when we consider the fact that while sweeping the celestial vaults with a powerful telescope, vast fields of nebulæ, like the Milky Way, burst upon our astonished and enraptured vision, revealing an infinite multiplicity of worlds, so vastly distant as to beggar all efforts of astronomical instruments to disintegrate the nebulæ and individualize the rolling worlds and blazing

suns, countless systems, wheeling their precipitate flight
in their appointed orbits through the immensity of track-
less ether, encircling the throne of God, responsive to the
Omnific mandate, overwhelming us with paradoxes and
astounding us with the irresistible conclusion that even
these one billion, one hundred and seventy millions of
worlds constitute but the suburbs of the celestial universe, fills and thrills us with bounding and irrepressi-
ble enthusiasm to spread the pinions of transfiguration
glory and fly away on the long anticipated tours of exploring with enraptured wonder the glories of Omnipotence.

CHAPTER II.

Ephesians, chapter 1, and Collossians 1 both vividly reveal our wonderful Christ in the redemption of this world and the confirmation of all worlds. In Eph. 1:10 we have *anakeptalairosasthai,* from *Ana,* again, and *keptale,* the head; therefore it means "to rehead all things in Christ, which are in the heavens and upon the earth." Hence you see that the work of Christ is not only for the restoration of the divine government in this world, but to restore all irregularities in other worlds, so confirming them in their allegiance to the divine government as forever to remove the probability of defection. Hence we see that the work of Christ is for the restoration of this world and the confirmation of all other worlds. The presumption that all of these worlds are inhabited by immortal intelligences is not only tenable, but very plausible. Hence, when we contemplate the infinitude of the celestial universe, the multitudes of angels inhabiting these boundless dominions must transcend all human apprehension and beggar every thought of enumeration. Doubtless many of these worlds are now in a chaotic state of progressive development, while multitudes of them have reached the higher achievements of celestial glorification, having been occupied by angels millions of ages.

CHAPTER III.

THE FALL OF LUCIFER.

Isa. 14:12: "How thou art fallen, O Lucifer, the son of the morning."

Lucifer means light-bearer, indicative of the brilliancy and splendor which radiated from the glory of this archangel. "And he said unto them, I was seeing Satan, having fallen like lightning out of heaven." Luke 10:18. The statement of our Savior certainly alludes to Satan's ejectment out of heaven, Lucifer having been his honorable archangelic cognomen, which infelicitously he exchanged for the odious epithet, Satan, which means adversary, from the fact that his glory had evanesced, his brilliancy departed, darkness supervened, accompanied by inveterate odium to the Almighty. Milton thinks it is because he ventured to aspire to the glory which God had in reservation for His Son. "And the Fifth angel sounded; and I saw a star having fallen out of heaven into the earth ,and the key of the bottomless pit was given unto him." Here John, in the apocaliptic visions, sees this star (Lucifer), who has become Satan, and has in his possession the key of the bottomless pit, showing that he has received the kingdom of hell and is ruling over it. Here we see that he opens the pit of the abyss *ad libitum;* hence we see that he exchanged the bright glories of the archangel for a kingdom in the black regions of endless woe. Milton and others, with no little plausibility, predicate their hypothesis of Lucifer's rivalry with the Son of God on Rev. 12, where we see the woman (the church) flying before the great red dragon, who was ready to devour her offspring (the Messiah). The Archangel Michael comes to her relief with an army of angels, fights against the dragon, defeats him and casts him out. Even after his signal defeat and ejectment, with uncompromising pertinacity, he continues to pursue the woman and wage war against her seed.

CHAPTER IV.

The presumption is that all immortal intelligences are like man, created on probation. Second Peter 2:4 tells us about "the angels wh ofell," and Jude 6 mentions "the angels who kept not their first estate"; while Rev. 12:4 tells us that the dragon's tail drew away "on-third of the stars of heaven and cast them down to the earth." "Stars" here means angels, and the dragon's tail means his influence, involving the conclusion that the fatal influence of Satan, the great archangel Lucifer, drew after him one-third of the angels and cast them down.

While dictating these pages, my emanuensis asks me if the angels are still falling, and if there is danger of the redeemed saints falling after they get to heaven. Of course, if successful to enter into heavenly glory, we shall never fall, from the simple fact that we have our probation here, which closes with this mortal life. As the angels never had mortal bodies, they pass through a probation in their immortal state—how long we know not; but sufficient for their ample testing and discipline. Doubtless many of the angels have already passed their probation. I trow there are many bright, celestial worlds in which you would not find a solitary probationer; i. e., no one there liable to fall. Yet it is highly probable, and I doubt not there are many heavenly worlds this day occupied by immortal intelligences on probation, lia-

8

ble to fall; and we know not how many of them do fall. The idea that we shall spend eternity unemployed is certainly very improbable. I trow when God takes me out of this world, He will have more use for me in some other. Why not send me to preach to the newly created inhabitants of some new-born world and fortify them against the apostasy which has turned this world into a graveyard?

CHAPTER V.

For the incarceration of the incorrigible subjects of His universal empire. There could be no such a thing as virtue without responsibility; and no responsibility without liberty; and no liberty without the possibility of the contrary choice. The removal of individuality would simply mean our dehumanization ,and the reduction of men and angels to the level of the inanimate creation. The Hebrew Sheol and the Greek Hades, which are perfectly synonymous in both Testaments, simply mean the unseen world which all enter at death, consequently these words include both heaven and hell. The rich man and Lazarus (Luke 16) both went into Hades, but we find them there under infinitely different environments; the latter tormented in the fires, and the former basking in the infinite delights of that intermediate paradise called "Abraham's Bosom," whither all the O. T. saints were gathered till the crucifixion of Christ consummated the redemptive scheme, verifying the Abrahamic covenant by sealing it with the precious blood of the vicarious atonement.

The annihilation dogma involves absurdity *ab initio*, committing the egregious blunder of materializing the soul as if it were a compound constituted of parts and susceptible of disintegration. The very fact that the soul is a unit, proves its indissolubility; unlike the body,

which contains sixty-two distinct chemical elements,
held together by the vital forces, despite the warring antagonism of the chemical, which speedily superinduce
putrification and disintegration on the relaxation of the
life principle.   The annihilationists commit the blunder of confounding life and existence, and death and
non-existence.   As physical death has no such meaning
as annihilation, but simply separation from life; existence real and actual continuing uninterrupted; so spiritual death simply means separation from God, who is
spiritual life, existence continuing indefinitely as real as
ever.   Annihilation is false in the material world, having
not a solitary illustrative example anywhere which is
irresistible, corroborative proof of the Scriptures, which
constantly proclaim the soul's immortality.   When Lucifer fell, he forfeited the divine life, but existed without interruption, perpetuating his identity, though in a
state of spiritual death.   Even so with all the angels.
The moment they separated their faithful allegiance and
identity with God, spiritual life evanesced, succeeded by
the woeful and doleful doom of spiritual death.   As they
followed Lucifer in his fatal apostasy and rebellion,
there was no place for them but the gloomy abyss, over
which omnipotence appointed him king (Rev. 9:12.),
giving him the key, and permitting him there to reign,
with his myrmidons and innumerable subordinates.

CHAPTER VI.

Not only do Peter, Jude, Isaiah and Jesus tell us about their fall, but John (Rev. 12) informs us that one-third of the heavenly host fell. This is really a vast number and an awful wreckage, as there is no redemption for them, since they were all adults and sinned personally; unlike the human race, who only sinned seminally, as they were all created in Adam and incurred the fatal collapse with him, having never committed personal transgression. When we consider the presumptive evidences of the infinite multiplicity of the angels and recognize the fact that the archangel Lucifer was transformed into Satan, Diabolus, the dragon, the old serpent, by the fall, it follows as a logical sequence that all the fallen angels following in his fatal trend became demons. These demons in the English Version are uniformly denominated "devils," demon being the correct word as you see in the Revised Version. We find Satan their great leader and commander-in-chief, recognized as "the prince of the power of the air," the spirit that now works in the children of disobedience; thus involving the conclusion that these innumerable demons constitute great armies bivouacked in the atmosphere, and rushing hither and thither in their enterprises, and waging devastating wars for the ruin of the human race. Satan is the originator of all human wars, sending out his innumerable myrmidons; he stirs up the dark demoniacal passions of men, precipitating the nations into deadly conflict, all to satisfy their hellish malice in the wholesale destruction of millions amid the precipitate storms of war without time for preparation to die, thus with the greatest possible rapidity populating hell. The New Testament constantly represents these demons as the uncompromising enemies of the human race. It is not important to give citations, you are witnesses to the patent fact. They are represented as enemies to the body, causing blindness, deafness, dumbness, lunacy, epilepsy, and a vast variety of terrible physical ailments, simultaneously so polluting the human spirit with an endless diversity of dark passions, brutal lusts and diabolical tempers that they are constantly denominated by the significant adjective "unclean," the loathsome leprosy and other appalling physical disorders but symbolizing the hellish venom with which they diabolized the souls of the people.

The innumerable eleemosynary institutions at the present day take in the victims of these evil spirits; otherwise the whole country would be overrun and terrorized by them as in the days of Christ. We have cases now illustrating the miraculous power of Christ to save from all these terrible disorders of the human race, and especially those belonging to the spiritual realm. The case of the Gadarene, who had a whole legion of these demons, i. e., ten thousand, illustrates the immense number which thronged that country in the days of Christ. The facts warrant the conclusion that not only is hell full of these tormentors, but the earth is inundated with them. The Old Testament as well as the New, abounds in references to them. The Israelites were not allowed to have anything to do with wizzards, witches, fortune-tellers, and practitioners of ledgerdemain. They were not allowed even to let them live among them, as the whole heathen world was full of them.

When I traveled in Africa and Asia among the Mohammedans, I met the magicians on all sides. It really seemed that they all knew how to work magic, and did their best to induce me to pay them money to perform miracles. In this country we have them on all sides—Spiritualists, Christian Scientists, hypnotists, astrologers, theosophists, and new parties ever and anon calling our attention to something on the line of the ancient sorcery, magic and withcraft. You may ignore it and pass it by as a sheer hoax and nothing in it. In this you are sadly mistaken. It is an immense and an awful reality. We are living in the midst of multitudinous excarnate spirits. Some able authorities claim that the disembodied spirits of the wicked, having become demons, are permitted to return to this world. This view would offer some plausibility to the claims of spiritualists to communicate with the departed. Some eminent Christian theologians favor this view. I do not think it is very tenable, as we can easily answer all the arguments of the Spiritualists on the hypothesis of these demons who are innumerable and everywhere, and taking so much interest in human affairs, laboring so assiduously for the destruction of all souls, that you will always find some of them on the spot and ready with a response to the call of the Spiritualists, whether true or false.

It is a perfectly reliable and indisputable fact, that

any person who will may come in contact with the invisible world and hold communion with them.   From the universal prevalence of these demons has originated the hypothesis of Satan's omnipresence, which is not true, as he is a finite being, and can exist only in one place at a time.   As we see from our Savior's testimony, Luke 10:18, that he has the power of locomotion at lightning speed.   Therefore, as lightning moves with a rapidity sufficient to go around the world fifty times in a minute, Satan can move from place to place with such rapidity as to beggar all recognition and superinduce the popular impression of his omnipresence, which belongs to no finite being, but to God alone.

CHAPTER VII.

"But those things which they sacrifice unto demons and not to God; I do not wish you to be the communicants of demons. You are not able to drink the cup of the Lord and of the table of demons; you are not able to partake of the Lord and of the table of demons." 1 Cor. 10:20, 21.

Here we find that the Greeks and Romans in the days of Paul worshipped demons. This word *daimonian*—demon—was constantly used to designate the various gods worshipped by the different heathen nations in the apostolic age. As we see in Rev. 12, Satan with his hosts fought against the archangel Michael and his heavenly army to defeat the plan of salvation in the beginning, when it was first projected and inaugurated. He has been on the battlefield ever since, though signally defeated by Michael and his army. We see in Dan. 12, that Michael with his celestial hosts will come to this world again at the end of the present age, and arrest the devil and take him out of the world and lock him up in hell, thus clearing the way for the ushering in of the glorious millennium. With God one day is as a thousand years (2 Pet. 3:8). When the bright day of Eden passed into the dark eclipse of the fall, God's glorious Sabbath was superceded by the black week of toil and burden, contrastively denominated night. Rom. 13:12:

"The night is far spent and the day draweth nigh."
Oh! how pertinently and significantly these six thousand
years of Satan's reign are by the Holy Spirit denominated night, in contrast with the blooming Eden which
preceded and the glorious Millennium destined to follow! Through all the six thousand years of Satan's
reign on the earth, he has pressed the battle with a zeal,
energy and indefatigability which we would all do well
to emulate. He has laid under contribution his wonderful archangel intellect to counterfeit and defeat everything God has done. He so captured the antediluvian
world as to cut down the Lord's people to a solitary
family, thus precipitating the divine intervention of the
flood, as the only possible prevention of the wholesale
damnation of all coming generations.

Though the world began anew, with no wicked people
on it, he launched his enterprises so adroitly as soon to
capture the post-diluvians, thus signally defeating the
patriarchal dispensation, running it into heathenism—
this day furnishing him about one thousand millions of
devout worshipers. Then he so captured Judaism as to
make the children of Abraham, the heirs of the promises,
kill their own Savior and sweep pell-mell into the abyss;
fallen Judaism and Mohammedanism, its magnitudi-
nous conterfeit, this day furnishing two hundred and
fifty millions of Satanic worshipers.

Then he so manipulated as to defeat the Apostolic
church, and run it into Roman Catholicism, which is
semi-paganism, and with her two hundred and fifty
millions, contains multituds of devout devil-worshipers.

One of the omens of the last days, is the rapid and

fatal apostasy of the Protestant churches which are alarmingly going over to Satan, and superinducing the necessity of the great Holiness Movement to utilize the surviving forces of the faithful few, in preaching the gospel to the ends of the earth, fulfilling the prophecies and preparing the elect for our coming King.

CHAPTER VIII.

As these demons are infinitely numerous, thronging the whole earth and sweeping in great armies through the air; hell, the loathsome dreary abyss, dreaded even by devils, being their head-quarters; therefore they are all anxious for a dwelling place on earth, nothing being so congenial to them as a human soul; therefore they are described as wandering over the earth seeking a resting place in some human spirit, so exceedingly numerous that frequently a whole troop crowd into one soul; the same person giving lodgment to a lying demon, a blaspheming demon, a demon of anger, another of lust, another of theft, and still another of pride, as we find Mary Magdalene had seven demons, till Jesus, in condescending mercy cast them all out, and called her to the gospel ministry, making her the recipient of signal and glorious graces and imperishable honors, last at the cross, first at the sepulchre, and first to receive the glorious commission of the full-orbed gospel, and first to go and preach the risen Jesus to the sorrowing disciples and a dying world. Of course these demoniacal possessions are all sinners and generally of the darkest type. Many a home is a miniature hell because the mother has the demon of an uncontrollable temper, gets violently mad, abuses her children, and torments her husband, giving them all a prelude of coming damnation. How wretch-

ed that home where the one who ought to be the guardian
angel is really the guardian devil getting them all ready
for hell! A man is possessed by the demon of murder,
who has power to run him into a fit of anger and renders
him absolutely uncontrollable. He shows up the venom
of hell and the rage of devils till he imbues his hands
with the blood of his fellow.

Many an unsuspecting woman has married a fine
looking man, who, to her unspeakable horror, in due time
shows up an incarnate devil. The millions this day who
frequent saloons, brothels, and gambling hells, and many
others moving in respectable circles are possessed of demons. The peculiarity of demonized people, is not that
they are always ungenteel or necessarily rough; but that
they have uncontrollable tempers, passions and appetites,
the demon taking hold of them in time of temptation
and proving more than they can manage. O how wretch-
ed the condition when thus enslaved by a vile, filthy demon, who knows no mercy, but rushes his victim head-
long to hell, as this is their great and constant work on
earth, to make their poor servitors fit only for hell and
lead them to it. As in the days of Christ, He is the only
one who has power to cast out these demons as they are
too strong for human beings. This accounts for the
supernatural feats of power and activity performed by
men when in deadly conflict, they slay their fellows.
This demoniacal ejectment is all done in conversion, as
the idea of demonized Christians is utterly incorrect.
Since these demons are all "unclean spirits," they terri-
bly pollute the souls in which they dwell, especially when
they have long abode in a human spirit. The great work

of entire sanctification is indispensable to remove all the
debris, and expurgate the saved soul from all the vile
pollutions which inhere and survive the demoniacal ejectment.　This problem is nicely solved and beautifully
illustrated by our Savior in Matt. 12:43. "But when the
unclean spirit may go out from the man, he goes through
dry places seeking rest, and finds it not.　Then he says;
I will return into my house whence I came out.　And
having come he finds it empty and swept and beautified.
Then he goes and takes with him seven other spirits
worse than himself, and having come in they dwell there,
and the last state of that man is worse than the first."
This is very simple and plain.　A solitary devil, we know
not of what species, whether lust, passion, temper, theft,
murder. . . . has taken possession of this poor sinner
and drives him under whip and lash, perhaps making
him get drunk in spite of himself, as is true with millions.　Fortunately the man happens in a glorious revival
and gets blessedly saved, Jesus reaching down and casting out the vile demon, who now walks through dry
places, i. e., tramping round hunting a lodging in some
human spirit.　Finding no other in whom he succeeds
in effecting an entrance, weary and discouraged, turning
on his heel he says, "I'll go back to my own house;" perhaps I can succeed in capturing it again."　So now he
comes back to the same man out of whom he had been
cast, and finds him in a nice fix, his sins having been
swept out by the besom of the Holy Spirit in regeneration, and the house elegantly beautified with the shining
graces of the new creation.　He makes an effort to re-
enter, but signally fails.　Then he goes and secures the

co-operation of seven more demons more wicked than himself. The man yields to the irresistible force. They all enter and there abide. He not only gives way to his old besetting sin, but now taking off his old restraints from other sins, he gives way to the devil, plunges into the wave of vice and floats upon the strong current of iniquity, yielding to seven distinct courses of dark criminality instead of one. Here you see the awful and fatal apostasy of a soul for the obvious reason that he was not sanctified. You see when the ejected demon returned, while he found his own house "swept and garnished," he also found it "empty," i. e., without an inhabitant. While the man with the grave of a genuine, clear, conversion, proves more than a match for his old master who had long driven him under whip and lash in the way of drunkenness, licentiousness, theft, or some other evil course; when he went away and secured the co-operation of seven other demons more wicked than himself, the man gives up, and the dismal cohort of eight vile fiends from the bottomless pit, walk in, and O what an appalling hell-den does his soul become! Now remember the old ejected demon found this soul "empty." If the man had only moved forward into entire sanctification, receiving the blessed indwelling Comforter, he would not have been found "empty;" but the Holy Ghost would have been dwelling in him, master of the situation, and would have proved more than a match for those eight demons. Consequently the man instead of falling would have found an easy victory.

CHAPTER IX.

DEMONIACAL INFLUENCE.

As the grand enterprise of Satan through the co-operation of his multitudinous myrmidons is nothing less than the wreck, ruin, and damnation of every human soul; while the genuine regeneration of the Holy Ghost always settles the great question of demoniacal eject-ment, as the real children of God are gloriously saved from indwelling demons; yet it is a great mistake to think they give up their hellish enterprises when a soul is converted. On the contrary they as you see in the above example, when this one went off and secured the co-operation of seven others, bigger and stronger than himself, did not cease till he dragged the poor man into a miserable apostasy. So if you abide in regeneration, rest assured the battle with hell will wax hot; whereas if you go for entire sanc-tification ,the myrmidous will stir all hell to keep you out of Beulah Land and zig-zagging in the howling wilderness, till you bleach your bones on the burning sands. It is also pre-eminently true as illustrated in the case of our Savior, when He received the Holy Ghost at the Jordan, Satan forthwith attacked Him in person. When you get thoroughly sanctified, these demons who have been angels and consequently well know how to play the angel, will array themselves as angels of light and impose themselves upon you, to your detriment and ruin.

These minions of the pit, cunningly manipulate all conceivable devices to allure you after popularity, office, and secular as well as ecclesiastical agrandizements, drawing on little by little, till they get you away from God and into darkness; then augmenting your delusion by the phosphorescent glare of hell's *ignis fatuus,* whose delusive ray lights up unreal worlds and glows but to betray. Oh, how potent these demoniacal influences against the preachers! Satan will commission a whole plattoon from hell to work night and day with one preacher, puff him up with vanity, inflate him with egotism, illure him with gold, buy him with ecclesiastical honors and seduce him with church preferment. These demons will actually monopolize his intellect, make sermons for him, help him to preach them, instructing him in pulpit and social etiquette. I am so sorry for the preachers. Many of them are actually spending their lives in a miniature hell, because of these demons who beset them in cohorts, assaults them in plattoons, never let up, till the devil getes a bill-of-sale of them, and they sink to the awful doom of meeting their own members in the black regions of irretrievable woe, where they will execrate them through all eternity with the burning odium of their damnation, because they softened the things which God made hard and smoothed the things which He made rough, thus permitting the people to slip through their fingers into hell.

There is really but one available attitude for a preacher or any Christian; and that is entire sanctification. When you receive the genuine article, then go on and get established in it; you are where the fiery darts of the enemy are all quenched the moment they strike your shield of faith; thus falling harmless at your feet. The indefatigable perseverance of Satan and his emissaries, is highly worthy of our commendation. Well has Jesus said, "The children of this world are wiser in their generation than the children of light."

After you have been truly sanctified and filled with the Holy Spirit, utilizing and appreciating the graces of establishment, invigoration, spiritual growth, and settlement in God, 1 Pet. 5:10, instead of hauling off his forces, Satan continues to detach more and yet wiser myrmidons from the pandemonium, never relaxing his determination in some way or other to catch your soul with his hellish lasso, and wreck you in the end. There is this eminently, constantly, and thrillingly consolatory fact that the panoply with which the Holy Ghost wants to invest you not only renders you invulnerable, but actually immortal. It is your glorious privilege to get where you can shout the victory night and day amid the hottest fire of the enemy, actually seeking the hottest of the fight, enjoying it so much the more, because you know that Satan is wasting all of his ammunition. The people who dread the assaults of earth and hell and are looking after easy places; so much need to go down deeper into God, and to get where they want the hottest fire, and the thickest of the fight. Oh, what a glory it is, actually daily and hourly to be proof against the artillery of hell, all the machinations of Satan, the culminations and devices of the world! Reader, are you there? Let the Holy Ghost have His way, and He will put you there.

CHAPTER X.

As these demons are so much more numerous than the whole human race and so inflexibly persistent in their determinations to throw the damnation lasso around every soul in all the world and in the finale populate hell with the whole human race; they never desist from their temptations. The more grace you have and the less the probability of your perdition, the more indefatigable they are. I heard of a man who enjoyed an optical view of the unseen world. He rises one morning and concludes to spend that day, hunting devils. He first goes to the race track where a great crowd of desperately wicked people were assembled and running the poor horses to death to satisfy their thieving crave for filthy lucre. He thought as he went along, "Surely I shall find a host of devils on those grounds." To his unutterable surprise, looking all around, he discovers not a solitary demon. He looks again more minutely feeling sure there must be a lot of them on the ground, carrying on that business. Eventually, looking out beneath a great spreading beech tree, he sees a solitary devil, sitting on a log so sleepy that he is about to fall off. The man halts and soliloquizes; "Satan in the exercise of his mature judgment concluded that one devil could manage all that crowd, and consequently dispatched him alone from the pandemonium to run that business which was fraught with so much interest to his kingdom."

On arrival, the devil found them all at their post, drinking whisky, cursing, swearing, gambling, fighting, and doing everything his Satanic Majesty could wish. Consequently having no job, he had gone away, sat down and just about to fall over into a profound lethean slumber. Then he goes on his way hunting devils, and comes along where an old hardshell Baptist, who had got religion when a youth and imbibed the doctrine of the final perseverance of the saints, not only believing it, but practicing the same. To his surprise he found there a vast multitude of devils. What was the solution? The old fellow was plowing a piece of new ground where the beech trees had stood thick, and their roots had monopolized the soil, the plow went jumping, sticking fast, anon breaking traces, singletree, hamestrings and smashing up things generally, tearing out great roots which would fly back and crack the old fellow's shins. Amid all he had the victory in his soul, shouted Hallelujah as he plowed along, and when his horse needed rest caught a little time to read his Bible. Hear the simple exegesis of the whole matter. The grave conclave in the pandemonium had dispatched a solitary devil to the spot to provoke the old saint and get him out of humor. He filled him so signally with a loud hallelujah roaring out of his wide-open mouth that he winged his flight back to the pit and reported; "No go." Of course they dispatched a regularly organized cohort, with a clerical fugleman not only to provoke him, but to conciliate him that he is justifiable in getting mad under the circumstances. He is still on fire and shouts them all out of countenance. With characteristic indefatigability, the wise peers of the pit now send a plattoon, who share the fate of their predecessors and report, "No go." Now they send a regiment, who are forced to acquiesce in the sad defeat of their predecessors. Finally they send a legion, who do their best on the temptation line, as they could really do nothing but talk to him, because God Almighty had rendered him not only immortal, but invulnerable; meanwhile the old saint finds all the assaults of hell but blessings in disguise, giving his soul, an unprecedented heavenly boom, and verifying that scripture so prominent in his creed, Rom. 8:28, "All things work together for good to them who love God, who are the called according to his purpose." Satan is not fool enough to waste his ammunition on dead game. He always shoots to kill.

In the ante-bellum days an old millionaire in the cotton states had great confidence in black Tom, who waited on his person and drove his carriage, running over with religion and often shouting aloud when on duty about the barnyard. As the old man was skeptical and hard, he often twitted Tom about his religion. Driving along through the piny woods on a summer day, he said: "Tom, why does the devil fight you so much? he never fights me. I have no trouble with him." Says Tom, "Massa, you must wait till de Lawd tells me and then I'll 'splain it." In a moment the master, looking out over a great pond, espies a flock of ducks, fires on them with his shotgun, being very fond of sport, killing one dead and crippling another, the rest all flying away; simultaneously shouting, "Run, Tom, and catch that duck." In a moment Tom dashes into the pond and catches the cripple duck which was fluttering on the water, and of course brings out the dead one, though nothing had been said about it. Dropping them down at their feet and driving on he says: "Now, Massa, I'll 'splain your question, why de devil gits after me, but never bodders you." Pointing at it with his finger, "Massa, you's dat dead duck, but I's de live one, and dat is de reason why de devil never shoots at you." Satan wastes no ammunition on sinners who are going to hell at race-horse speed. Neither does he expend much ammunition on people in the justified state, as he knows they will backslide and finally wind up in hell, if they do not go on into holiness. But when you get truly sanctified, then he lays under contribution all the resources of pandemonium to intimidate, disturb, sidetrack, derail, entangle, or upset you in some way. It is after you have been sanctified wholly and entered into this glorious soul rest, that you learn to fight the good fight of faith. The sinner is frequently actuated by noble aspirations to be good; ever and anon when under the powerful conviction of the Holy Spirit, he resolves over and over to quit all his sins and seek the Lord. But he is an alien from God and a stranger to grace, and consequently makes a thousand good resolutions, relying on his own resources, destined to speedy failure and crushing collapse, going into deeper despair and down farther and farther into the devouring vortex of sin. After he is converted and becomes a Christian soldier, he prosecutes a mixed warfare against the devil; himself and Jesus doing the fighting. Anon leaning too much on the former, the latter lets him go and he receives the profitable discipline of an awful cudgeling by the triumphant adversary. But the glorious work of entire sanctification exterminates self, brings Jesus to the front, making Him sole Arbiter of your destiny for time and eternity. Henceforth you rest sweetly in His arms and He fights all your battles for you and wins a glorious victory in every assault by the enemy. Sanctified faith does not fight its own battles, but abides in perfect rest, simply holding Jesus by the hand who does all the fighting for you. Faith is the grace which receives and holds on. Hence this is fighting the good fight of faith. You rest delectably in the arms of Jesus, who does all your fighting for you. In the epistle to Ephesians we have much said about "heavenly places." That letter gives the highest type of spirituality in the Bible. But we find in the last chapter a vivid portrayal of the terrible battles fought even in those heavenly places.

"Put on the panoply of God that you may be able to stand against the methods of the devil, because there is not to us fighting against blood and flesh but against governments, against authorities, against the world rulers of this darkness, against wicked spirits in the heavenlies. Therefore take the panoply of God in order that you may be able to stand in the evil day and having done all things to stand." You observe in the E.V. "places" italicised, showing that it is not in the original, the true meaning of *epouranios* being simply the "heavenlies." The experience of entire sanctification, utterly destroying the carnal mind and filling you with the Holy Ghost, puts you out into the heavenlies, i. e., into the heavenly state, in which your graces of perfect submission to the Divine will, perfect faith, love, and obedience are really homogeneous with those enjoyed by the saints in glory. Yet you are in this wicked world, on the battlefield, encompassed by the hosts of hell, who are certain never to let up till you pass through the pearly portals. "Wiles" is *methodias* and means methods, because Satan has ways, plans, schemes, stratagems, and expedients numberless to defeat and destroy every soul in this world. At this you are not surprised, because he claims this world, and is grossly insulted at the slightest insinuation impeaching his sovereign rights and royal dignity. This is not all simply his own infatuation, 2 Cor. 4:4. God calls him "the god of this age," not as the E. V. has it "this world," which would imply his perpetual dominion over the world. For reasons we have neither time nor space here to expound, Satan is permitted to rule the world during the present age, while God is calling out the Bride of Christ to reign with Him eternally, an honored participant in the glorious administration of celestial worlds. Therefore we are living during the black reign of Satan on the earth, destined to wind up with the present age, when the archangel will arrest him, and lock him up in hell, forever putting an end to his dominion on the earth. In this same exhortation Paul specifies the different weapons of our warfare, among which the shield of faith is conspicuous, assuring us that it will quench all the fiery darts of the enemy. The word quench literally means to put the fire out as when the engines pour a flood of water on a burning building. Here we find that Satan shoots at the saints

even in their heavenly experiences of entire sanctification, sending his missiles thick and fast, flaming with
hell fire. But you see the shield of faith not only ar-
rests all the missiles, but actually puts all the fire out,
resulting in no harm to the saints, but awful damage to
the devil who loses all his ammunition, thus bank-
rupting hell. Hence you see the normal state of this
exterminating warfare waged against the saints uninter-
mittingly, till they go to glory. You must ask
the Lord to reveal to you this grand lesson
of constant fighting, incessant victory, and perfect rest at the same time. The great solution of the
matter is, Jesus does all your fighting for you, leaving
you nothing to do, but rest at his feet, shout and be true.
While a sinner there is but one side to the war, for Satan
whips you all the time, having an easy victory; in the
justified experience the war is mixed on your side, yourself and Jesus fighting the devil. But in the experience
of entire sanctification, it is no longer yourself; you died
on the cross and fight no more. You're lost in Jesus,
singing as you go:

> "I have found a friend in Jesus,
> He is everything to me,
> The fairest of ten thousand to my soul;
> The Lily of the valley, in him alone I see.
> All I need to make and keep me fully whole;
> "He all my griefs has taken,
> And all my sorrows borne,
> In temptation, He's my strong and mighty tower;
> I've all for Him forsaken,
> And all my idols torn from my heart,
> And now He keeps me by His power."

As you have sunk away into God, you have really gotten to where the devil can't find you, and never will again; yet he keeps on shooting where he thinks you are, only to waste all his ammunition.

Perfect love makes you so brave that neither men nor devils can scare you. You soon find that you're utterly out of danger, and must fall in love with the battlefield, having gotten to where James says "Count it all joy, my brethren, when you fall into manifold temptations, knowing the trial of your faith works out patience. And let patience have its perfect work in order that you may be perfect and whole in every part lacking in nothing." Since every temptation opens a fight with the devil, and you've nothing to do, but turn it over to Jesus and shout the victory, receiving a great blessing by way of establishing you in the triumphant graces of entire sanctification; only be steadfast and the time will soon come when you will fall much in love with the war, preferring the front of the battle and the thickest of the fight; like Job's war horse, of which he said, "He smelleth the battle afar off." So you become literally fond of the battle-field and can smell it afar off, and pursuant to your acute spiritual olfactories, hunt it up. "But each one is tempted by his own lust being drawn out and enticed; then lust conceiving brings forth sin, and sin having been made perfect brings forth death." This is a temptation which none of us should have; it comes from within and is exceedingly dangerous; fraught with defeat and spiritual death. Sanctification takes this lust out of you,expurgating it by the cleansing blood and burning it up with the fires of the Holy Ghost. Many lions may roar around you, while you are safe in your impregnable stone mansion, and they can do nothing but roar, for they cannot get in to hurt you. But suppose you have one lion in your house, he is very likely to eat you up for his next breakfast. Hence we see that the great danger is from temptations that come from within, no amount of merely external antagonism being competent to hurt you, except it is reciprocated and co-operated by the internal. Bunyan's Pilgrim, while traveling along the King's highway, was almost constantly assaulted by giants, monsters, and devils. On one occasion Bunyan says he became awfully perplexed when encompassed by a multitude of Satanic emissaries, who crowded around him, and some of them got in position behind his ear where they whispered awful blasphemies, till poor Pilgrim almost concluded that they were coming out of his own heart, and became much grieved. Let us profit by this example of demoniacal temptation. A man asked me yesterday, "What is the difference between thinking evil and thinking of evil?" The difference is as wide as the universe. You cannot live in this world, which is full of evil and not think of it. There is no sin in thinking of evil; but when you think evil in your heart you commit sin. "Man looks on the outside, but God looks on the heart" and reads our thoughts. Since we are literally encompassed by these demons, whose grand enterprise is the importation of evil to our minds and everything they can possibly do to secure and expedite our ruin; you'll never reach a state in this world in which these demons will not suggest evil, as in case of Pilgrim. They spoke awful blasphemies and did their best to persuade him that they came out of his own heart. These evil spirits actually talk to you, uttering blasphemous, obscene, rebellious, and awful things. When you go out among wicked people you are compelled to hear profanity, ribaldry, and debasing follies. Of course you're not responsible, from the simple fact that you cannot prevent that state of things. Even so these demons, who fill the air, crowd around you and actually utter abominable things in your spiritual ears, thus taking advantage of every little mishap, disappointment, mistake, and interruption, that chances to cross your path, quicker than you can think, precipitating evil utterances into your mind and vile communications into your ears. Then the demon thus haunting you, will turn and accuse you of all these evil things which himself has suggested, and face you down that they originated in your own heart, and in that way discourage you and get you under a cloud. Let me here warn you of Satan's ladder. It contains six steps which lead down to hell, everyone beginning with D, in harmony with devil.

Doubt.
Discouragement.
Despondency
Despair.
Death (spiritual)
Damnation.

I give this specification for your profitable warning. If you don't want to go to hell, be sure you keep off the devil's ladder. You begin with doubt, then become despondent and get discouraged, going on into a chronic case of the blues, developing into actual despair, giving up your hope,final apostasy which is spiritual death, sealing your unhappy fate till heaven, hope, and salvation are gone into eternal eclipse, these demons, your old enemies, drag you into hell and consign you to damnation world without end.

CHAPTER XI.

The meaning of this caption is simply "led away by a demon." These demons have all been angels and consequently understand how to play the angel and thus counterfeit the Holy Ghost. This is their fond caprice with holiness people, pursuant to which many are constantly getting deflected away, going into wild fanaticism, getting tilted off into a diversity of "isms" and "scisms," derailed, side-tracked and ditched, till their usefulness is paralyzed. How shall I stand against the fearful liabilities encompassing me on all sides while these demons with ten thousand seductive and plausible arguments are doing their utmost to run me off on a tangent, destroy my usefulness and, if possible, wreck and ruin my soul? There is just one grand and impregnable fortification against all these diabolical intrigues, and that is the Divine leadership.

Man is a trinity, consisting of spirit, mind and body. Divine leadership is adapted to us in these three great departments of our trinitarian constitution. The Holy Spirit is the Divinely appointed leader of my spirit; the Word the grand school for the culture and development of my immortal mind, while God's providence, encompassing my material being on all sides, furnishes constant guidance for my body. If we give the preponderant attention to the providences which appertain to the body, there is danger of becoming deistical and materialistic in our views. If we study the word alone, without due appreciation of the Spirit and providence, there is danger of drifting away into dead formality, drying up, becoming creedistic, theoretical, and unspiritual; while in the case of preponderant adhesion to the leadership of the Spirit, there is danger of drifting away into fanaticism. These three great departments of the Divine leadership are to be appreciated proportionately and symmetrically. When I climbed the Egyptian pyramid, which covers thirteen acres of ground, and is five hundred and fifty feet high, doubtless having been built by the ante-diluvians, the greatest superstructure of human hands in all the world; as the enterprise was somewhat perilous, I secured the assistance of three Bedouin Arabs active as catamounts, one taking each hand and the other pushing me from the rear as I ascended. With these strong and elastic porters, I I went directly up the pyramid. I could go no other way; as it was impossible to go to the right or to the left, or to stop in my ascension. I give this by way of illustrating the greatest of all enterprises, i. e., our climbing up to heaven.

By the providence of God I mean your present environments. God created you and put you where you are. You're to be true to all your opportunities for reception and dispensation, i. e., get all the good you can, and do all the good you can. You've no right to close a door of usefulness, which God has opened. Are you born a Methodist? there is an open door to do good among those people. You can reach your own sect, nationality and color, perhaps more successfully than any other person. So let us all enter every door which God opens, glorifying Him by witnessing to His mercy, grace and power to save. The Bible is so wonderfully voluminous, revealing every ramification of Divine truth and every phase of duty and responsibility, if you'll study it with reasonable diligence, you can find out your whole duty to God and man. There is really no subject, theme nor enterprise on which you are likely to embark, but you have ample information in the blessed Book of Truth. It will enlighten your immortal intellect and fortify you against the side-tracking intrigues of the enemy. It is your glorious privilege to receive the illumination, regeneration, sanctification, consolation, and guidance of the blessed Holy Spirit, who will keep you in communion with God, making you a constant participant of heavenly manna, thus permitting you to feast on angel's food to which the world is a stranger. This tripple leadership of the Lord, is your ample and abundant fortification against all the demoniacal devices of the infernal world. The climacteric policy of these adroit and cunning demons is to get you very zealous about following the Holy Ghost. Now remember, the Bible no where tells you to follow the Holy Ghost, but constantly urges you to follow Jesus. Well, what is the difference? None in fact, but a great deal in doctrine. As Jesus has a human body, and has been born, lived, and died in this world; and we have His biography by four inspired authors, lest we might make a mistake in our efforts to follow Him, therefore we are all left without excuse, as to the glorious feasibility of following Jesus. Not so in reference to our attempts to follow the Holy Ghost. He has no human body, no incarnation. Consequently we are unable to utilize and appropriate His personal character in our daily lives. He is ever to us a profound and indissoluble mystery. From the simple fact that He has no incarnation, these evil spirits who are also excarnate can counterfeit Him and pass themselves off under His cognomen. Not so with Jesus; as He has a human body, it is impossible for any demon to counterfeit Him and pass himself off on you for Christ. Therefore the perpetual safeguard against these constant liabilities of being led astray by evil spirits, is simply to put your eye on Jesus, walk steadfastly in His foot prints. So long as your eye is on Him, His hand is on you and it is impossible for men and devils to tilt you up or deflect you from the way; meanwhile you also enjoy the leadership of the Holy Spirit, because His mission unto the world is to reveal Jesus to the spiritual eye, and at the same time to give you all the grace which you need to follow Him. While we are no where commanded to follow the Holy Ghost, we are assured that so many as are led by the Spirit of God the same are the sons of God, and the Spirit himself bears witness that we are the children of God, Rom. 8:15, Hence you see the indwelling Holy Spirit, His guidance, and leadership, and witness to our adoption, clearly and abundantly revealed in the blessed Word. Hence the attitude of the true Christian is beautiful and glorious in the extreme, holding Jesus by the hand, the Holy Ghost filling you and witnessing to your adoption, and His sweet, blessed, copious and wonderful words instructing your immortal intellect, feeding your

soul, enabling you to grow from babyhood into giant-
hood, ready for the glorious transfiguration when the
Lord appears. Therefore you see this tripple leadership of the Lord is really all the panoply you need, im-
pregnably to fortify you against all the machinations of
earth and hell, carried on by incarnate devils in the form
of wicked men and women, and excarnate devils through
the agency of these innumerable demons, who fill the air
and are always ready to seduce a soul; for they linger
along beside the King's highway of holiness, like lightning hanging on the skirts of the clouds, ready every moment to leap on you, stun, perplex, and stagger you, or
illure, enchant, seduce, or entangle you. Satan is not
much concerned about the millions of dead professors, as
he knows the probabilities all favor their damnation.
But he is awfully concerned about the people who go for
holiness with all the power of soul, mind, and body. He
knows he must do something quickly or give them up
forever. O, how busy millions of demons are working
night and day to sidetrack the holiness people. John
Wesley warns us constantly against enthusiasm. The
English language has undergone some changes since his
day, fanaticism now meaning what enthusiasm did in
the days of Wesley. You must not be afraid they will
call you a fanatic. Remember perfect love casts out
fear and puts you where you are ready for the reproach
of Christ, and willing to be called fanatic, crazy, fool,
or anything else for His sake. You may expect these
opprobrious epithets. If you have not sufficient holy
zeal to make dead professors and the wicked people of
the world call you a fanatic, you ought to be alarmed

over your spiritual condition; I greatly fear the devil is close on your track, and if you do not stir up and make a new departure in your Christian experience, he will get you yet. N. B. It is one thing to be called a fanatic and quite another to be a fanatic. They said of Jesus, "He has a demon;" "He is gone mad;" "He is beside Himself." The servant is not above his Lord. You may expect to have a diversity of odious epithets heaped on you.

They are included in your consecration and will not hurt you. Rejoice in them, but do not seek them. This does not change the fact that fanaticism is really the work of these demons, who are so fond of passing themselves for the Holy Ghost, and leading you away step by step, until they get you into darkness and finally land you in hell. Hence I would warn you, with Wesley; "Beware of fanaticism." There is much of it on all sides; take heed and govern yourselves accordingly. We're living in the "perilious times" of which we are warned in the latter day prophecies. This booklet with all of my writings is dedicated to the holiness people in all lands. Glory to God forever. Amen.

THE DEVIL AND DEMONS.

There is a great deal of confusion in the minds of Bible readers on this subject. Our common version of the Scriptures increases the confusion rather than diminishes it. Here we read of "devils" being cast out of men, when it should be "demons." Properly speaking, there is but one devil, whereas demons may be numbered by hundreds of millions. We know that a legion of the demons were cast out of one man. Satan himself is the arch-enemy of God and man. He is known by various names in the Scriptures. He is called Abaddon in Hebrew, Apollyon in Greek, and the meaning is "destroyer" (Rev. 9:11). He is called "the angel of the bottomless pit,' "'the accuser of the brethren" (Rev. 12:10), "the adversary" (1 Pet. 5:8), "Beelzebub, the prince of devils" (Matt. 12:24), "the great dragon" (Rev. 12:7, 9), "the god of this world" (2 Cor. 4:4), "prince of this world" (John 12:31), "prince of the power of the air" (Eph. 2:2), "the old serpent" (2 Cor. 11:3; Rev. 12:9), "the tempter" (1 Thess. 3:5), and "that wicked one" (Matt. 13:19; 1 John 2:13 and 5:19). All these titles, and yet others that might be given, are applied to the one great enemy, Satan. They are not applied to his underlings. These seem to have no personal names in Scripture, but are simply bunched and called "demons." I think it will be found on examination that in every instance where the word "devils" is used in the plural, the Greek has "demons."

It seems probable that most of our temptations come, not from the devil, but from demons. As there is but one Satan, and he is not omnipresent, he evidently could not attend in person to all men. He is, however, served by a strong force of allies who do his bidding and seek by every possible means the destruction of men.

Whether demon possession is common now as in the days of Jesus, we have no means of absolutely knowing. Bro. Godbey seems to favor the idea that demon possession continues as in the olden times. This may be true. If so, it may account for much of the drunkenness, the gambling, the murdering and thievery, the lewdness, and other kinds of wickedness that imperil our civilization. An understanding of this question would certainly be profitable, as Christian workers would know better how to grapple with the difficulties. It may be possible that lunacy and epilepsy are of demoniac origin. If so, he who can cast out the demons can rid us of these dire calamities. Men and women of faith should set themselves to the solving of this problem. It is worthy of prayer and thought. We know that when Jesus was on earth, he not only cast out demons himself, but empowered his disciples to do the same. He is the same yesterday, today and forever (Heb. 12:8). We suppose that demons have not changed, and human nature seems to be about the same. Why, therefore, might not the faithful disciples of the Lord perform in His name, and by His authority, the same deeds of power now as nineteen centuries ago? The power of the Christ is not diminished. The resistance of demons is perhaps no greater now than then. Faith was and is the weapon of victory (Matt. 17:20, 21; 1 John 5:4). The Master has even said, "According to your faith, be it done unto you."

As to Satan—he is the prince of demons, their generalissimo. His keen wit and far-seeing intelligence, with his next to omnipotent power, are at their service. They work through his power and under his direction. In one place we read of 200,000,000 of them turned loose on the earth at one time under his leadership (Rev. 9:16). We know that Satan is termed the "god of this age" (2 Cor. 4:4.) This seems to imply that the world as it now exists is under his infernal power and arrayed with him against the kingdom of Christ.

Few men who can consent to remain in sin have any conception of their own abject slavery to Beelzebub. But it is certainly true that sinners are under his power. (Acts 26:18.) Their redemption consists in annulling Satanic power and placing them under the guidance and support of the Almighty Spirit of God. Our warfare is against "rulers" and "wicked spirits" in heavenly places. (Eph. 6:12.) When a man consents to serve Satan, he has a hard master, and one whose hellish ingenuity will be brought to bear for the thorough demonization of his victim.

Satan was once an angel of light, burning and shining in celestial glory and evidently very near to the throne of God. He no doubt took high rank among the celestial hierarchy. All his skill and power seem to remain with him to this day.

In the book of Daniel we have an account of a time when the prophet went on a long fast, continuing three full weeks. There appeared to him an angel whose glory was marvelous. The description (Dan. 10:5-12) reminds one very much of the picture of Jesus himself as set forth in the first chapter of Revelation. The angel's glory was so excessive that the prophet fainted before it, and needed a touch divine to revive him. This glorious angel makes the following astounding announcement: "From the first day that thou didst set thy heart to understand, and to chasten thyself before thy God, thy words were heard, and I am come for thy words. But the prince of the kingdom of Persia withstood me one and twenty days; but, lo, Michael, one of the chief princes, came to help me." Thus it seems that even this glorious celestial being had a three-weeks' battle with Satan, for he is evidently the one intended by the term, "prince of the kingdom of Persia." It seems that the assistance of even Michael, the great arch-angel, was necessary that the battle might be won. Might not this case solve the question of the delayed answer to many of our prayers? Daniel's petition was heard at the beginning, but help did not reach him for three weeks because of the obstructions put in the angel's way by Satan. Is not a man very foolish to put his life into the service of such a dreaded foe as this? Why should one willingly sell out soul and body for time and eternity to one who is the greatest foe of his own best interests? Satan shall have no part in my life. Where we meet, it shall be on the battle-field. Demons do his bidding, and they, like him, are infernal in their character and conduct. He who is wise, will seek to be at once and forever freed from their presence and polluting power.

[Since writing the above I have read the following

from Rev. F. B. Meyer, of London, the noted Baptist preacher, and from Mrs. Baker, of Rochester, N. Y. The cases are so suitable to these pages that I give them space.]

L. L. PICKETT.

DEMON POSSESSION IN RUSSIA.

REV. F. B. MEYER.

[This article may throw some light by way of illustration on the subject under discussion.]

I want to narrate the essence of a most interesting conversation at the breakfast-table with Baron von Uexkull and others.

He introduced it by speaking of an Esthonian lady, a governess, who was called in to see a dying man. As she spoke of Christ he cursed, and refused to hear anything of the Gospel. To all appearance he died the same night. When she went to the house on the next day he was lying on the bed apparently dead. However, she felt impelled to lay her hands on him, with the result that he recovered animation, and awoke not only to consciousness, but to a devout faith in the Gospel, in which he died some six hours after. I do not quote this as an instance of raising one from the dead, because he might have been in a coma; but it is a remarkable incident, specially his reception of Jesus Christ.

There was another story told by a Christian physician, who has a house for the treatment of nervous diseases, of a little boy of six, who was brought to him as having tried to hang himself. The child said that as he was playing near his mother's house a man came to him and told him what he must do. Evidently this was a mere impression on the child's mind, as there was no man of the description about the place. The child seemed in constant dread of this person's returning, until prayer brought him peace.

The baron also told of a man of his acquaintance who occupied a farm on his estate, and who was under the power of what seemed to be a nervous disease. The baron asked him to kneel in prayer, and repeat the words of petition, after himself, which the young man did, until he came to the name of Jesus—this he refused to repeat. When the baron insisted on his saying it, and with a great effort he did so, he fell on the ground with a scream. The baron bade the evil spirit come forth, which it appeared to do, leaving the man exhausted but well.

A similar instance was related of an old and wealthy count, who was subject to fits of ungovernable passion, and was the terror of his wife and children. But when, in answer to definite prayer, God gave power to His servant to command the evil spirit to go forth, he became calm and gentle, and afterwards died in the full faith of Christ.

On one occasion Count Pashkoff, with some other believers, prayed for four hours for a man who was all the while mocking them, and saying that their efforts were useless, that there was not one demon only in possession, but many. Finally, when in despair, the count said, "Lord Jesus, we have no power at all to drive forth this evil spirit, do Thou do it," there was an evident going forth of some evil influence, and the man became subdued and quiet.

Another terrible incident was told me by the count

of a man whom he knew in the early days of his religious life, and whom the neighbors had imprisoned in a large iron cage, the bars being of terrific strength. And whenever any were brought in to see him, he held out towards them a silver rouble, saying, "This is my God, this is my God." I confess that these incidents have greatly impressed me. I wonder how far it would be right to deal with certain forms of impurity and drunkenness as being cases of demon-possession. It may be that there is more of this demon work among ourselves than we know, and specially in cases of mania. The baron told me that once, when visiting an asylum, there was a great movement among the patients on his entrance of the wards, as though thy recognized in him the power of the living Savior.

My friend, Baron Nicolai, also says that in his judgment there is a great difference between demon-influence and demon-possession; and reminds me that Dr. Howard Taylor has said that in China he was accustomed to diagnose the symptoms of demon-possession in the same way as of any other disease.

These things make me feel more and more the desire to be not only influenced, but possessed by the Holy Spirit. They invest the Day of Pentecost with an altogether new significance. It may be that the evil around us is to a larger extent than we have ever realized the result of the distinct operation of Satan and his agents, and therefore our one need is to seek such a mighty infilling and possession of the Spirit of God as that the power of the evil one may be cast out by a stronger.

A godly man in the town where I am writing these

words who is just now greatly afflicted, confesses to be always conscious of an evil spirit who is perpetually beside him, and is constantly denying the truth of Christianity, and the Deity and power of Christ. He has been a bright and useful servant of the Lord Jesus, until this has befallen him, and he is greatly tried by it. What depths of Satan there are! What mysterious influences may not be affecting the currents and movements of our time! We may be in the presence of mighty spiritual forces, which we are endeavoring to combat by wholly intellectual methods, forgetting that Spirit can cast out spirit.

I am passing no personal opinion on these matters. But it seems as if suddenly I had been brought into contact with the conditions of the early Church. Here again is the mighty power of divine manifestation, and here the forces of the evil one. They drive one to first principles, to read the Bible again from a new standpoint, and to pray to experience more and more the power of the Divine Spirit, that one may be able to cast out the spirits.—*London Christian.*

In connection with the above, we should like to mention a few cases which have come under our own observation in the past years of our contact with the sick and suffering.

The first case was that of a Christian man, wholly insane, yet whose friends were not willing to send to an asylum, as the family believed in the power of the Lord to heal. Whenever any one of them would enter his room, he would mock at them, with the most satanic leer upon his face, taunting them with the powerlessness of their God to heal him, telling them to call upon their God and let Him heal if He could, followed by mocking laughter. To remain in his presence became unbearable. One day when we were in his room praying with the family, the Lord said to me *"go and rebuke that evil spirit in him casting it out."*

"O! I cannot," I said, never having had to deal with such cases of demon-possession before. "I have not the power or the faith to do it. *"Do you believe in the power of My Name? Do you believe it has the same power as when I was on earth?"* He asked. "Yes, Lord," I replied. *"Then go and use it. You do not need to have faith in any power of your own, but in the power of My Name."* I arose, timidly to be sure, but with perfect confidence in the power of the name of Jesus (See Mark 16:17) and commanded the blaspheming spirit to come out, and found it instantly obeyed, for even the countenance altered, and the whole sickness changed from that hour.

The next case was that of a young lady suffering from melancholia, sent to us by a friend rather than to an asylum which was a last resort. The poor girl could do nothing when awake, but arraign the wisdom and government of God in the affairs of men, by constant questions, till one felt like running from the room. At other times she would lie for days in bed with her face buried in her hands, refusing to reply to anyone addressing her, or to rise. We prayed over her for days with no apparent results, when one day God shewed us that she was possessed with a demon which must be cast out before the healing could come. (There is no healing the devil.) We accordingly went to the bed where she was lying and one of our number in the name of Jesus commanded the evil spirit to come out of her. This was repeated several times, as we felt great resistance, when the demon left, and the girl arose and proved to be entirely delivered from all satanic power. She soon after gave her heart to God, and was admitted to full membership in one of our city churches, giving every evidence of a sound mind.

Another case was that of a little girl nine years old, who, her mother said, had been always so perverse, stubborn and ugly as to make her friends despair of ever being able to manage her. No discipline seemed to have the slightest effect. There seemed to be an unnatural hartlessness and cruelty about her that no amount of kindness could change.

She had been the subject of most earnest prayers for years and sometimes seemed touched, but only a transient impression was made upon her, which quickly passed away, leaving the old satanic meanness uppermost. The mother was a consecrated woman, but the father, though a professing Christian, was a wicked man. One day as we engaged in prayer with the mother, being in real despair over the child, it was shown us that she had been possessed with a stubborn, obstinate demon from her birth. We at once cried mightily to God for deliverance and in the name of Jesus commanded the spirit to leave her, which it did.

This was some time ago. The mother informs us that she is a changed child, all cruelty and stubbornness having left her from that hour, making her easy to govern.

Think of this little child, an unconscious tool in the hands of satan, through an evil spirit, used to bring pain, misery and constant disturbance and torment to the whole household, really wrecking her mother's health through the constant conflict; the little child herself suffering through her own powerless effort to be obedient, a power stronger than her will utterly controlling her. May not this be the explanation of many failures in parental government, and many lost and ruined lives of the children of even Christian parents, who have not lacked proper training?

Is it not time that we should read our Bible over again, as Mr. Meyer suggests, and awake to this awful conflict with the power of darkness all about us in the souls and bodies of men? May God give us an intelligent faith for such suffering ones.

Mrs. E. V. Baker.

THE DEVIL.

BY ANDREW JOHNSON, WILMORE, KY.

It has been taught in many colleges and universities
of our land, as well as from certain pulpits, that there is
no real, personal devil, but only wickedness in man, or a
personified spirit of evil. Against this unscriptural dogma we level the following Bible truths:

(1) *Personality of Satan.*—Satan was once a holy
angel in heaven; but through sin he wast cast out. Rev.
12:9; Isa. 14:12; Luke 10:18; 2 Peter 2:4; Jude 6.

The arguments ,then, that prove the angels are personal, intelligent beings, may be justly applied to Satan,
since through his fall, he did not lose his personality, but
simply the divine image.

(2) *Some Characteristics of the Devil.*—Presumption, Job 1:6, Matt. 4:5, 6. Pride, 1 Tim. 3:6. Power,
Eph. 2:2, Eph. 6:12. Deceit, 2 Cor. 11:14, Eph. 6:11.
Wickedness, 1 John 2:13. Fierceness and cruelty, Luke
8:29 and 9:39-42, 1 Peter 5:8. Malignancy, Job 1:9
and 2:4. Activity, Job 1:7 and 2:2. Cowardice, Jas.
4:7. Histories and encyclopedias abound with charac-
terizations of the world's heroes, poets, generals and
statesmen; but where can we find a more accurate delin-
eation of any character than that given of fallen Lucifer,
the arch-enemy, on the pages of the inspired Word?

(3) *Works of the Devil.*—He brought about the fall
of man (Gen. 3:1, 6, 14, 24). He endeavored also to
superinduce the fall of the Second Adam, but signally
failed (Matt. 4:3-10). His skill has been exerted in

wresting the Scriptures (Matt. 4:6 and Ps. 91:11, 12). When the angel appeared to array Joshua, the high priest (Zech 3:1), in clean garments, Satan was on the scene to resist. His diabolical ingenuity has not only put the filthy garments of sin about precious souls, but has hindered penitent seekers from becoming vested with the spotless robes of righteousness. But for Satan's power, the gospel would reap its thousands where it now only garners its tens or maybe scores from the fields of sin (Matt. 13:19; 2 Cor. 4:4).

The devil is now the god of this world (2 Cor. 4:4), and as humanity's insidious foe, he has done his most ingenious work along the line of beguiling unstable souls." He assumes the form of an angel of light (2 Cor. 11:4), and performs lying wonders (2 Thess. 2:9; Rev. 16:14). The ignis fatuus and the mirage in nature may deceive our physical sight, but the spiritual eyes of the whole world have been blinded by this deceiver. (Rev. 12:9). One has only to look at the great systems of false religion today to see how securely multitudes are held by the hand of the deceiver. Only those who have received the true gospel are delivered from the grasp of Satan's delusions.

(4) *Destiny of Satan.*—In Rev. 12:12, we read, "Woe to the inhabiters of the earth and of the sea; for the devil is come down unto you, having great wrath because he knoweth that he hath but a short time." Thus we see that the devil is doing his utmost in damning souls, for his time is limited and his doom is inevitable. As it has been with empires, so has it been with individuals. Greece and Rome rose to imperial zenith and sank

in ruins. This will be the fate of Lucifer. He has long been the prince of the ages, he has swayed his cruel scepter over the sons of Adam, but soon the apocalyptic angel, with chain in hand, will descend from heaven, dethrone Satan and consign him to the bottomless pit for a thousand years, during which time Christ, the rightful ruler, and His saints shall reign on earth (Rev. 20: 1-4; Rev. 5:10). After the thousand years have expired, Satan shall be loosed for a little season. His long imprisonment does not change his nature or quiet his animosity. He rallies his forces and compasses the beloved city, but the battle proves to be his Waterloo, and the lake of fire and brimstone becomes his eternal abode. Thus his eventful and awful career on earth ends, and amid the cruel flames he and all his followers are tormented day and night forever and ever. (Rev. 20:8-10.)

We also learn from the Bible that there are sub-devils, fiends or wicked spirits, as well as one chief Devil or Satan. Rev. 12:9 tells us that Lucifer's angels were cast out with him. Again, in Jude 6, it is stated that the angels (plural number) which kept not their first estate—he hath reserved in everlasting chains under darkness unto the judgment of the great day. By the power of Christ a legion of devils (demons, rather) were cast out of the demoniac (Mark 5:13), and Mary Magdalene had seven devils (demons) from which she was delivered by the grace of God. Hence we are encouraged, for since there is a reality in Satan and demons, yet Christ is Almighty and has triumphantly conquered them all, and in due time will banish them to their eternal doom.

AN ANGEL VISIT.

REV. J. M. DUSTMAN.

[Having so much in preceding pages on demons, it will be refreshing to our readers to have the following account of a visitant from the celestial world. I was rather skeptical of the facts at first glance. But as I read the plain, straight-forward story, so direct, so definite, and so full of detail, I was convinced that it is true, and herein submit it to our readers. Of course, if any one should write to Mrs. Hittle, a stamp (or more) should be enclosed. Doubtless many inquiries will result, and something should be allowed for the labor of answering.— L. L. P.]

"When they shall rise from the dead, they. . . . are as the angels which are in heaven."—Mark 12 :25.

For the glory of God and for the encouragement of his obedient children, I record this bit of marvelous history, which occurred in the month of February, A. D., 1887, in the northern part of Darke county, Ohio.

About three miles from the town of Possville, there lives a family by name of John and Hattie Hittle. They had six children, whose names and ages respectively were as follows: Ora, twelve; Henry, ten; Lizzie, eight; Ida, six; Nettie, four; and Pearly, two.

They were religious people, and enjoyed the blessing of entire sanctification. They were and are still members of the Massasinawa class of Greenville Mission of the Indiana Conference of the Evangelical Association. Their home has for many years been the home of the itinerant preachers.

There was a protracted meeting in progress in the neighborhood ,and the parents and Ora were going to the meeting, while the rest of the children were to stay at home alone. They had never stayed alone before, and therefore protested against it on the plea that they were afraid. But the mother told them not to be afraid, for God and the angels would take care of them.

Finally they consented, and after the parents were gone they lowered the blinds, locked the doors, and gathered together on the sofa to have their family worship. Pearly, however, had already been put to sleep in the cradle in the bed-room. After they had all said their prayers, they happened to get hold of Foster's Child's Story of the Bible, which had been presented to Ora on his twelfth birthday. They began to look at the pictures in it, and presently they came to the picture of an angel, whereupon Henry exclaimed, "O, I wish I could see an angel once!" And each one of the rest said, "I wish I could, too!" They had hardly said this when they heard some one stamp on the porch and knock at the door. So they all jumped up and ran to the door to see who was coming. They raised the curtain and looked out, and, behold! to their great surprise, an angel came right in through the glass and stood among them. His presence, however, did not in the least frighten them, for, they say, he looked so pleasant, and immediately began to talk to them. He asked them where their parents were, and they told him that they had gone to meeting. Then

Lizzie, who happened to be standing by the rocking-chair, said to him, "Take a chair and sit down." He answered, "O, I can't stay long." But he took the chair and drew it up toward the stove and sat down, saying as he did so, "You have a nice stove and a good warm fire." Then the children noticed that he was barefooted, and as the weather was quite cold and the ground was covered with snow, they would naturally suppose that he must have cold feet. Therefore Henry said to him, "Put your feet on the railing of the stove and warm them." The angel did so, and then called the children up to him. They, however, were still wondering in their minds why he should be barefooted in such cold weather, and this made them take particular notice of his feet, which, they say, looked perfectly white and glistened like wax. He then reached out his hands and drew them closer to him, and then raised them upon his knees, two on each knee, and caressed them by putting his arms around them, stroking their hair and laying his hands upon their heads as if he was blessing them. At the same time he kept talking to them all the while, and told them to be good children and not neglect to keep on praying to God, etc. They say his voice was clear and perfectly charming, his hair very fine and wavy, and he wore a beautiful little crown on his head.

After he had thus held them and talked to them for awhile he put them down again. And rising from the chair, he began to walk around in the room and looked at the pictures on the walls. And as he was walking around they noticed that his garment was loosely thrown around him and extended a little below his knees. It consisted of the finest white fabric, and rustled like leaves, or like silk, as he moved around. They could now also have a better opportunity to see his wings, which were quite large, and fairly glittered for whiteness. The children all followed him closely wherever he went, and presently they came to the bedroom where Pearly was sleeping. With the children still close at his side, he went to the cradle and took up Pearly in his arms and kissed her, and then laid her down again, saying as he did so, "When Pearly gets older you must tell her to be a good girl and pray, too." Then he said to them, "Well, I must go now," and began to shake hands with each one of them and thus bid them good-bye. And it is impossible to describe the loveliness of his hand as they took hold of it. It felt just like snow, or like a soft, downy cushion. And, like his feet, it was perfectly white and glistening. He wore a most heavenly smile upon his countenance. His voice was most tender and sweet. His entire demeanor was marked with gentleness and kindness, and his whole appearance was only that of grandeur and beauty. So that not only their fears were all banished, but they also felt perfectly at home and enraptured by his presence. And it really made them feel sad when he told them that he must go.

But after he had bidden them good-bye, he started immediately for the door through which he had come in, while the children were still standing at the bedroom door. When he came to the door he paused a moment and the children noticed that he had a long staff which he held horizontally in his hands, and in an instant they saw him gliding out through the unopened door in the same manner that he had come in.

As soon as they saw that he was gone, they instantly made a rush for the door, literally stumbling over one another to get there first, and when they got to it and had raised the curtain and were looking out, they saw him standing on the edge of the porch and a bright cloud had gathered around him. Then they saw him glide out into the yard. His body was now in an inclined position, with his feet extending backward and his wings partially unfolded, while the lower part of his garment and the bright cloud seemed to roll and fold themselves together in a most unique manner. He went on in this way until he came about half way between the house and a pear tree, which was standing in the yard, and then he ascended upward, and the last they saw of him was his beautiful white feet. Then one of the children exclaimed, "Now he is gone!" and another said, "I wonder why there was no bright cloud around him while he was with us in the room," and still another said, "I wonder how long it will take him to get to heaven?"

And the next thing in order was to wait until the return of the parents and Ora, that they might tell it to them. They could scarcely wait until they came, they were so anxious to tell them. In the meantime they carefully examined the door from top to bottom, rubbing their hands over it, to see if there was not a crack or a break of some kind where he had come in and gone out. But to their atosnishment they could not find the least sign of a crack, either on the door, the glass, or on the casing of the door. After awhile they heard their parents coming, and they were all up and ready to meet them. The mother went to the house first, while the father and Ora put away the team. But who can imagine the bustle and excitement which ensued as the mother entered the house. Henry, Lizzie, Ida and Nettie, each one trying to tell it first. They jumped, they laughed, they clapped their hands, and were perfectly wild with joy. So great was the noise and holy racket that the father and Ora heard them at the barn, and wondered what in the world was the matter with the children.

"Who do you suppose was here, mother, while you was gone?" they all exclaimed with one accord. "An angel, yes, an angel. O mother, an angel was here." And then when the mother had quieted them sufficiently, they went on to describe him, how he looked, what he had done, and what he had said.

Their shining faces, their exultant spirits, their positive declarations and the unison of their assertions, soon overwhelmingly convinced the mother of the truthfulness of her children's story, and of the reality of the vision which they had seen. Besides, being a spiritual woman and having an insight into spiritual things, she could all the more easily be persuaded of the facts in the case. She listened to them with suppressed emotions until her heart could no longer contain the joy which filled and thrilled her whole being. Then, going to the bedroom, she threw herself upon the bed and gave vent to her feelings with loud shouts of Glory to God. She felt that the very house was hallowed by the presence of the Lord, and that from henceforth more than ever, her home should be like a little heaven on earth. After arising from the bed, she seated herself in a chair near the stove and buried her face in her hands.

Presently the father and Ora returned from the barn, and as they entered the room where she was sitting she exclaimed, "O, father, you ought to hear the children tell of the wonderful visitor which they had while we were gone!" whereupon the children began to tell the story to their father and older brother. "Ah," said the father, "you are only excited, it was simply your imagination. You did not see an angel." "Yes, yes, father; sure, sure," came from every one of them. And so positive were they and still so overwhelmingly happy, that the father could not long withstand their simple arguments, but was compelled to believe that what they were telling him was true, and soon he also began to praise the Lord, and to participate in their joy.

This simple story has been told by this dear family to only a few of their most intimate friends. They deem it too sacred to be told to everybody, as everybody could not appreciate it. The writer became their pastor in the spring of 1896, and not until the evening of January 7, 1897, did they tell me about it; and the way it came about was this: Ida and Nettie had been to school during the day and the question came up whether or not the Lord revealed himself to men now as he did in olden times through the ministry of angels, etc. The teacher seemed to be somewhat skeptical, and said he did not believe such things were possible at the present time. He had, however, never heard of this instance, and therefore knew nothing about it until Ida declared her belief in such things from the fact that they had seen an **angel**

in their home when they were children. So when she
came home from school she was telling her mother what
the teacher had said, and how she had convinced him
contrary to his former belief. I happened to overhear
their conversation and began to wonder what they were
talking about. Then they happened to think that they
had never told me the story yet, and at once began to
relate it to me. And as the children were all at home,
they were soon all seated around me, and with shining
faces, were busily engaged in making known to me this
most remarkable incident. And it has made an impression upon me that shall never leave me. And while they
were telling me I felt that such a good thing as this
should not be kept a secret any longer. Therefore, on
the day following, I wrote out a minute history of the
same, just as the children had told me. Of course they
were no longer little children, but all except Pearly had
grown up to be young men and young women.

The reader may imagine what a thrill of joy and
gladness filled my soul while, by the help of God, I, for
the first time, undertook to write this story. Here I
was in the very room where it had all occurred. To my
left was the same sofa upon which these children had
their family worship on that memorable night in February, ten years before. A little farther on to my left was
the very door through which he had come in and gone
out. To my right was the same rocking-chair in which
this heavenly messenger had been seated. In my lap
lay the same book, opened at the very picture which had
brought from them the wish that they might see an

angel once. And upstairs is the stove which he said was so nice.

Nearly five years later (November 27, 1901), I visited them again. All the children except Ora are still at home, and in the evening while seated with them in this same room, and talking to them about the matter, I found that after the lapse of nearly fifteen years it has not in the least lost any of its freshness in their memories. For with shining faces, and with hearts glowing with gratitude to God for His great goodness to them, they still love to talk about the wonderful visitor which He, in His kind providence, had seen fit to send to them in the days of their childhood. Their whole lives have been influenced by it, and I told them that when I shall meet them in glory in company with their angel friend, I should like to have a talk with them concerning this matter.

Surely "The angel of the Lord encampeth round about them that fear Him and delivereth them."—Ps. 34 :7.

"And the angel of His presence saved them." Isa. 63 :9. "An angel from heaven strengthened Him." Luke 22 :43. "Who maketh his angels spirits and his ministers a flame of fire." Heb. 1 :7. "Are they not all ministering spirits, sent forth to minister for them who shall be heirs of salvation." Heb. 1 :14.

If, after reading this story, any of my readers should doubt the veracity of it, I would direct you to write to the family yourselves. Write to Mrs. Hattie Hittle, Hagerman P. O., Darke county, O., and I am certain that you will receive a prompt and kindly reply.

Hoping that these lines will prove a great blessing to many hearts by strengthening their faith in God's holy Word and promises, and that they will draw the reader very near to the blessed Savior, who has promised soon to come in the glory of His Father, with all His holy angels. Let us not be ashamed to own Him before this wicked world, and thus compel Him to be ashamed of us before the angels of God. But let us forsake every evil way, and yield our all to Him by entire consecration and faith, and He will not only pardon our sins, but will also cleanse us from all unrighteousness. Then in the morning of the first resurrection we shall not only be as the angels which are in heaven, but we shall be like our blessed Redeemer who has washed us from our sins in His own blood, and has made us kings and priests unto God.

Urbana, Ind.

THE EXPLODED DEVIL.

Men don't believe in a devil now,
　As their fathers used to do;
They have opened the door of the widest creed
　To let His Majesty through,
And there isn't a print of his cloven foot,
　Nor a fiery dart from his bow
To be found in earth or air to-day,
　For the world has voted it so.

But who is mixing the terrible draught
　That palsies the heart and brain?

Who loads the bier of each passing year
  With ten hundred thousand slain?
Who blights the bloom of the earth to-day
  With the fiery breath of hell,
If the devil isn't and never was,
  Won't somebody rise and tell?

Who dogs the steps of the toiling saint?
  Who digs the pit for his feet?
Who sows the tares in the field of time
  Wherever God sows the wheat?
The devil is voted not to be,
  And of course the thing is true;
But who is doing the terrible work
  Which the devil alone should do?

We're told that he does not go about
  Like a roaring lion now,
But whom shall we hold responsible
  For the everlasting row
To be heard in church and state to-day,
  To earth's remotest bound,
If the devil by unanimous vote
  Is nowhere to be found?

Won't somebody step to the front forthwith,
  And make his bow and show
How the frauds and crimes of a single day
  Spring up? we'd like to know.
The devil is voted not to be,
  And of course the devil's gone,
But simple people would like to know
  Who carries his business on?
                    —*Rev. Alfred J. Hough.*